صَاحَت وَالِدَتُهَا : " فِي الْمَطْبَخِ طَعَامٌ كَثِيرٌ . "
" وَلَكِنْ لاَ تَأْكُلِي مِنَ الْفِلْفِلَةِ الْحَمْرَاءِ الْحَرَّاقَةِ . "

"Plenty of food in the kitchen!" shouted her mother.
"But don't eat the red hot chilli!"

فَذَهَبَتْ لِيمَا إِلَي اُلْمَطْبَخِ لِتلُوكَ شَيْئاً .
فَوَجَدَت جَوزَةَ هِنْد بُنِّيَّة وَبِهَا شَعْرٌ كَثِير .
وَلَكِنَّهَا كَانَت حَقًّا جَامِدَةً جِدّاً عَلَيْهَا .

So Lima went to the kitchen for a nibble,

She found a hairy brown coconut
But it was just ... too hard.

وَالسَّامُوسَاتُ اللاَّمِعَة
كَانَتْ قد بَرُدَت جِدّاً.

The shiny samosas
Were just ... too cold.

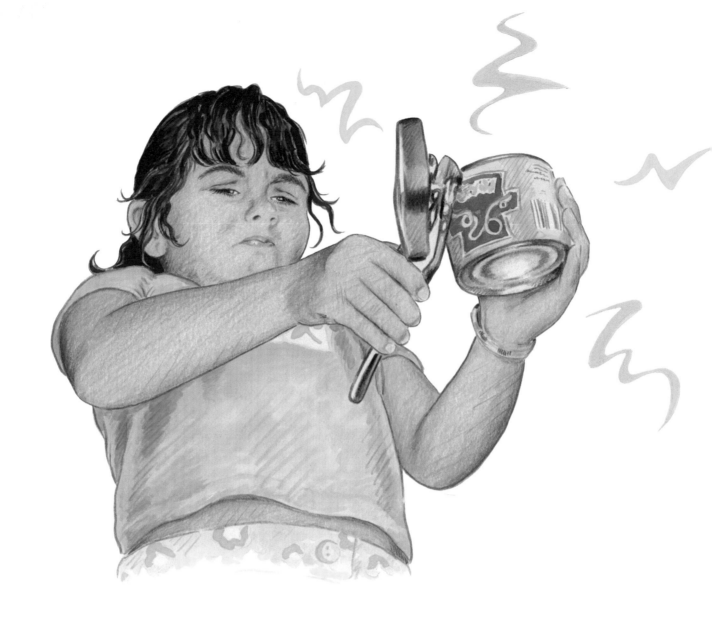

وَعِلْبَةُ الْمَكَرُونَة
كَانَتْ حَقًّا ... صَعْبَةً عَلَيْهَا أَنْ تَفْتَحَهَا.

The can of spaghetti
Was just ... too difficult.

وَالْحَلْوَيَاتُ اَللَّزِجَة
كَانَتْ بِالْفِعْلِ . . . أَعْلَي مِن لِيمَا .

And the sticky sweets
Were just ... too high up for Lima.

ثُمَّ رَأَتْهَا .
الشَّيْىُ . . . الأَلَذُّ الأَلْمَعُ الأَحْمَرُ!
الْفِلْفِلَةُ الْحَمْرَاءُ الْحَرَّاقة .

Then she saw it.
The most delicious, shiny, red ... thing!
The RED HOT CHILLI.

بِهُدُوءٍ وَدُونَ أَنْ يَرَاهَا أَحَد.
وَضَعَتْهَا لِيمَا فِي فَمِهَا.

Quietly and secretly
Lima popped it into her mouth.

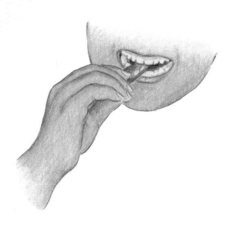

فَقَرْقَشَتْ!

Crunch!

وَلَمْ تَسْتَطِعْ أَنْ تُحَافِظ عَلَي سِرِّهَا طَويلاً

But she could not keep her secret
very long!

أَصْبَحَ وَجْهُ لِيمَا أَحَرَّ
وَأَحَرَّ وَأَحَرَّ وَ...

Lima's face got hotter
and hotter and hotter and...

... طَارَتْ أَلْعَابٌ نَارِيَّةٌ مِنْ فَمِهَا !

...fireworks flew out of her mouth!

جَاءَتْ وَالِدَتُهَا لِكَي تُسَاعِد.
"اُلْمَاء، اُلْمَاء، جَرِّبِي بَعْضَ اُلْمَاء. "

Her Mother came to help.
"Water, water, try some water!"

فَابْتَلَعَتْ لِيمَا كُوبًا كَامِلاً مِنَ اُلْمَاءِ اُلْبَارِدِ اُلْبَارِدِ .
وَكَانَ لَطِيفًا . . .
وَلكِنْ مَا زَالَ فَمُهَا حَارّاً جِدّاً !

So Lima swallowed a whole glass of cold cold water
Which was nice ...
But her mouth was still too hot!

ثُمَّ جَاءَ وَالِدُهَا لِكَي يُسَاعِد.
"أيس كريم، أيس كريم، جَرِّبِي بَعْضَ أيس كريم!"

Then her Dad came to help.
"Ice cream, ice cream, try some ice cream!"

فَأَكَلَتْ لِيمَا مَلاَعِقَ مِنَ الأَيس كريم اَلْمُثَلَّج
وَكَانَ جَمِيلاً. . .
وَلكِنْ مَا زَالَ فَمُهَا حَارّاً جِدّاً!

So Lima ate dollops of freezing ice cream
Which was lovely ...
But her mouth was still too hot!

ثُمَّ جَاءَتْ خَالَتُهَا لِكَي تُسَاعِد.
"جلي ، جلي ، جَرِّبي بَعْضَ الْجلي !"

Then her Aunty came to help.
"Jelly, jelly, try some jelly!"

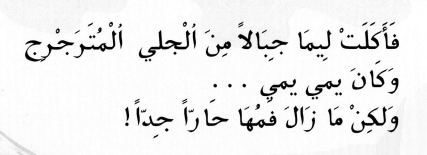

فَأَكَلَتْ لِيمَا جِبَالاً مِنَ الْجِلي الْمُتَرَجْرِج
وَكَانَ يمِي يمِي . . .
وَلَكِنْ مَا زَالَ فمُهَا حَارّاً جِدّاً!

So Lima ate mountains of wobbly jelly
Which was yummy ...
But her mouth was still too hot!

ثُمَّ جَاءَ جدُّهَا لِكَي يُسَاعِد.
"مَنْجُو، مَنْجُو، جَرِّبِي بَعْضَ اَلْمَنْجُو!"

Then her Grandad came to help.
"Mango, mango, try some mango!"

فَأَكَلَتْ لِيمَا حَبَّةً كَامِلَةً مِنَ الْمَنْجُو الْمَلِيئَة بِالْعَصِيرِ
وَكَانَت لَذِيذَةً. . .
وَلَكِنْ مَا زَالَ فَمُهَا حَارًّا جِدّاً!

So Lima ate a whole juicy mango
Which was delicious ...
But her mouth was still too hot!

أَخيراً جَاءَتْ جِدَّتُهَا لِكَي تُسَاعِد.
"حَلِيب، حَلِيب، جَرِّبِي بَعْضَ الْحَلِيب!"

At last her Grandma came to help.
"Milk, milk, try some milk!"

فَشَرِبَتْ لِيمَا إِبْرِيقًا كَبِيراً مِنَ الْحَلِيب الْبَارِد.
بِبُطْئٍ شَدِيد ...

So Lima drank a huge jug of cool milk.
Then slowly ...

اِبْتَسَمَتْ لِيمَا بَسْمَةً صَافِيَة .
وَقَالَت "أَاااااااه! تُبْتُ مِنِ الْفِلْفِلِ الْأَحْمَرَ الْحَارّ."
"تَنَهَّدَ" الْجَمِيعُ.

Lima smiled a milky smile.
"Ahhhh!" said Lima. "No more red hot chilli."
"Phew!" said everyone.

”وَالآنَ،“ قَالَتْ وَالِدَةُ لِيمَا، ”هَلْ مَا زِلْتِ جَوْعَانَة؟“
”لاَ،“ قَالَتْ لِيمَا مَاسِكَةً بَطْنَهَا. ”بَس شوية مليَانة!“

"Now," said Lima's Mum, "are you still hungry?"
"No," said Lima, holding her belly. "Just a bit full!"

For Lima, who inspired the story
D.M.

To all the Brazells and Mireskandaris,
especially Shadi, Babak & Jaleh, with love
D.B.

First published in 1999 by Mantra Lingua Ltd
Global House, 303 Ballards Lane, London N12 8NP
www. mantralingua.com

Text copyright © David Mills 1999
Illustrations copyright © Derek Brazell 1999
Dual language text copyright © 1999 Mantra Lingua
Audio copyright © 2011 Mantra Lingua

This sound enabled edition published 2013